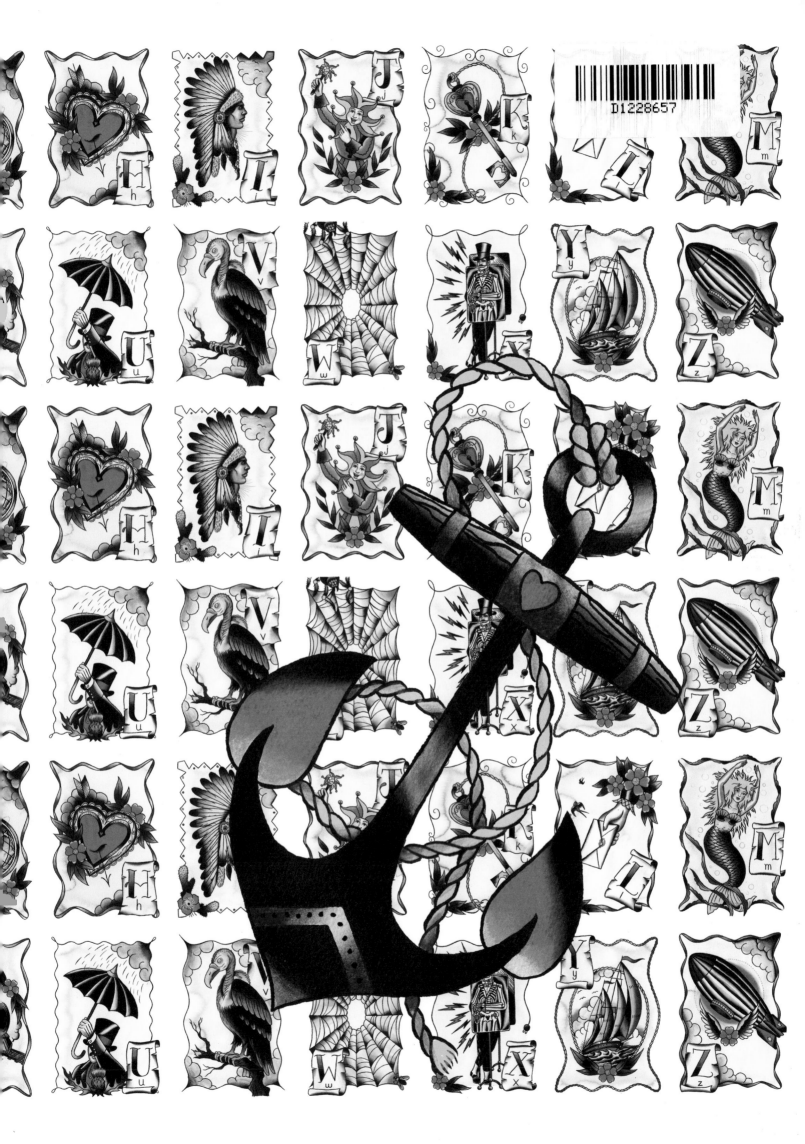

PAUL SLIFER'S

A IS FOR ANCHOR

AN ILLUSTRATED ALPHABET INSPIRED BY DESIGNS FROM TRADITIONAL WESTERN TATTOO ART

Schiffer Publishing Ltd

4880 Lower Valley Road • Atglen, PA 19310

d IS FOR DRAGON, WISDOM, LUCK AND MIGHT

e IS FOR EAGLE, ALL IN A FLAP

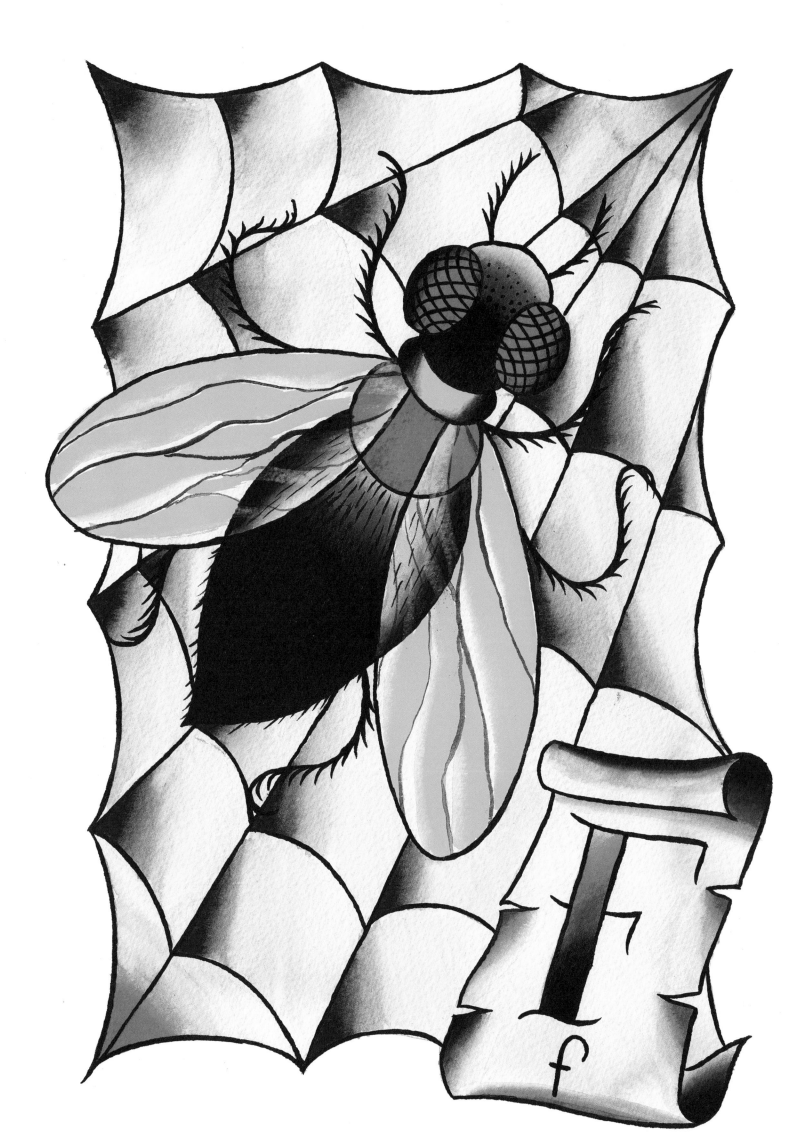

q IS FOR QUEEN, SYMBOLISING EVERY MOTHER

r IS FOR ROSE, THE QUINTESSENTIAL FLOWER

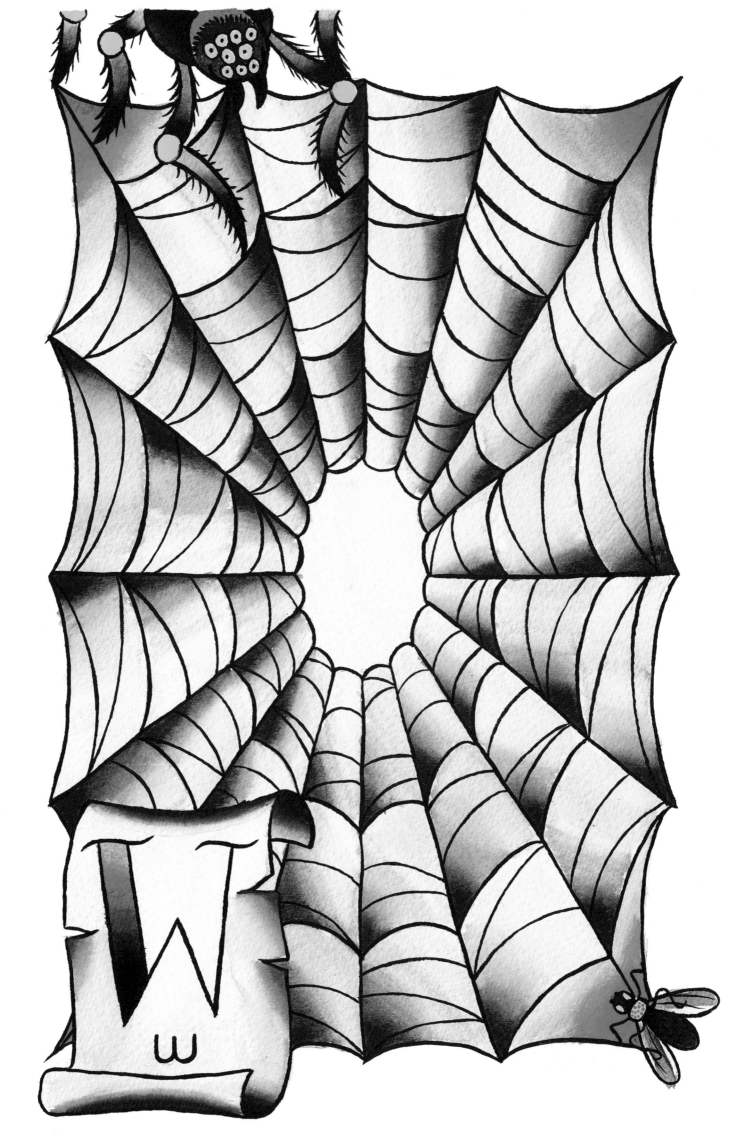

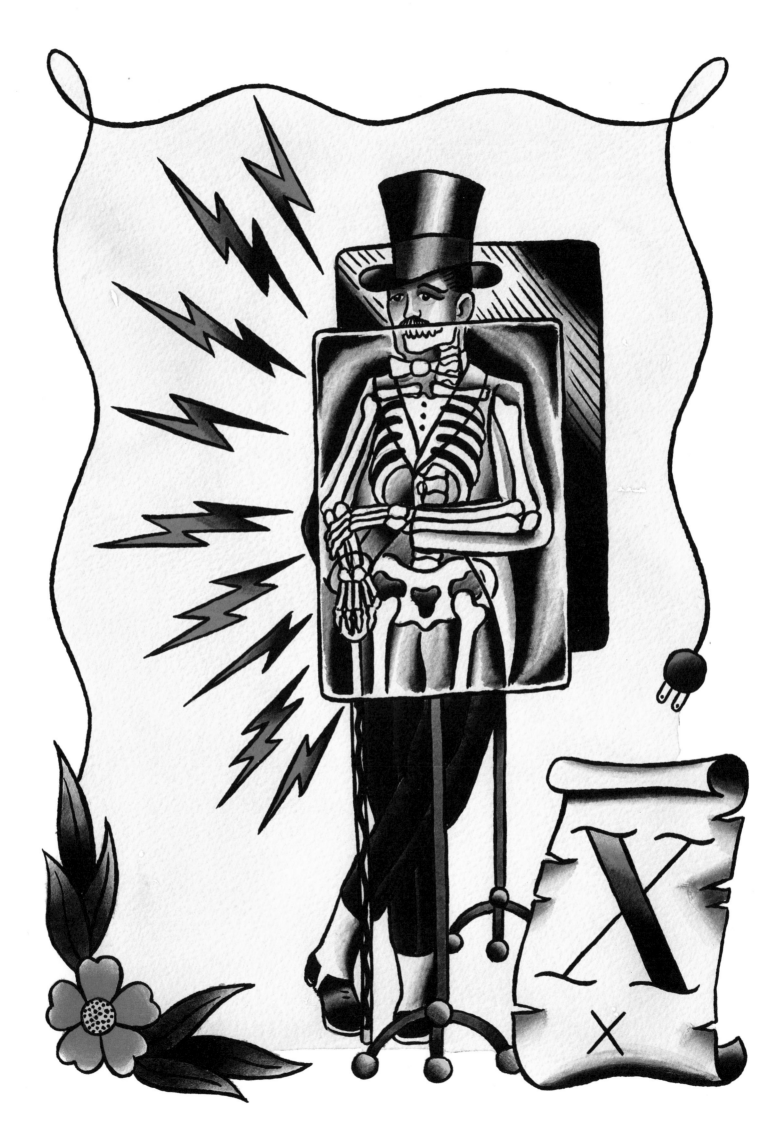

X IS FOR
X-RAY
A RADIOACTIVE
SCAN

Z